Technical Analysis Techniques For Timing The Market And Trend Trading

ISBN 1451516797
EAN 978-1-451-51679-1

1. Hedge-Fund 2. Hedgefund 3. Derivatives 4. ETF
5. Exchange-Traded-Fund 6. Options 7. Investing
8. Strategies 9. Trading 10. Day-Trading
11. Technical-Analysis 12. Charting 13. Bollinger-Bands
13. MACD 14. Stochastic

Printed in the United States of America

DESCRIPTION AND EXPLANATION
Of
Technical Analysis Techniques For Timing The Market And Trend Trading

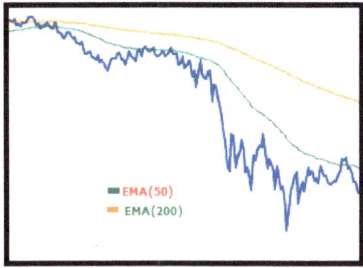 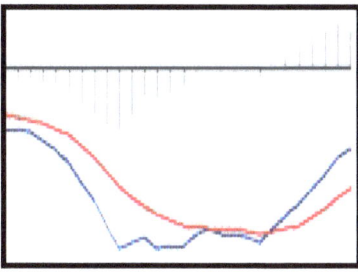 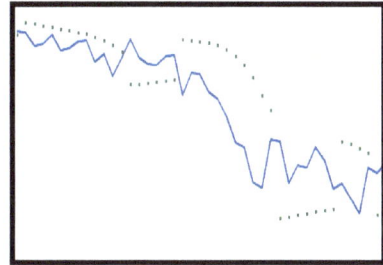

It should not be assumed that these techniques will be accurate in the future or will equal the performance of the examples as explained in this newsletter.

Singularly, one person or institution does not have the power to change the direction of the market. Market direction trends are reversed only by people and institutions acting as a group. The signals that tell them to buy or sell are visual interpretations of market data presented in the form of graphs and charts called technical indicators. Trained investors monitor these technical indicators, in addition to global credit conditions, recession cycles and option market hedging activity. It is important for the average investor to understand technical indicators in order to develop their own short term and long term investing strategies comparable to those employed by professional traders and hedge funds.

What Is An Investment?
An investment is a security that has been purchased to be sold at a higher price in the hope of realizing a profit. A fixed-income investment, commonly known as a bond, is a security that is purchased, held over a specified period of time while receiving regular interest payments (sometimes combined with the repayment of the invested amount, i.e., the principal) until the time period ends, and the invested amount is returned to the investor. Investments are a net drain on monies, because profits (if available) are not realized until the investment is sold. Buying an investment is also termed *long*, e.g.: The investor went long 100 shares of AT&T stock.

What Is A Position?
A position is an investment in reverse. It is sold first at a market price and then purchased back at a lower price, resulting in a profit from the actions of selling high and buying low. Profits are received immediately in a position. Losses can occur if the position moves in an adverse direction. Buying a position is also termed *short*, e.g.: The investor went short 100 shares of MCI stock.

What Is A Hedge?

A hedge is an act, tool or means of preventing loss of investment principal or position profit with a partially or fully counter-balancing security.

What Is Leverage?

Leverage is the process of reducing the investment amount to achieve an increase in the return. An investment amount is reduced by applying monies from other sources (such as through a loan) that lower the required investment amount while maintaining the profit amount. A further explanation of leverage must include the difference between a return and a yield. A return is profit divided by the investment amount. For example, if a $100 investment can realize a profit of $10, the return is $10 ÷ $100 = 10%. The return number can be increased by lowering the investment amount through leverage. So, if a $100 investment only required that $90 of the $100 be used to earn a profit of $10, the return is $10 ÷ $90 = 11%. However, by using leverage or leveraging the investment amount, the return percentage is now defined as the yield, a return that has applied leverage to its investment.

What Is A Stop Loss?

A stop loss is an instruction attached to an investment or position to sell, in the case of the investment, or to buy, in the case of the position, to prevent or limit losses resulting from adverse price movements.

What Is Technical Analysis?

Technical analysis is the deciphering of market data for the purpose of anticipating and identifying asset price trends and predicting asset price movements.

What Is Trend Trading?

Trend trading is the timed entry into or exit out of an investment or position based on a security's trend (bullish or bearish) as determined by technical analysis.

What Are The Ways To Profit From Market Timing?

Profiting from market timing is a function of establishing an investment or position just prior to or immediately after a favorable price movement in the underlying security. All price movements are favorable when one has the ability to invest, position and hedge.

.

What Are The Risks? What Are The Rewards?

The risk in market timing is that sometimes the readings technical indicators provide are inaccurate, resulting in the placement of an incorrect investment or position order. This incorrect placement will result in a loss unless abated through the use of a stop loss or a hedge. The reward in market timing is the opportunity to establish an investment or position that profits from correctly anticipated movements of underlying securities, selling when the price movement has achieved a cycle high and buying when the price movement has achieved a cycle low.

Technical Indicators For Timing The Market And Trend Trading

There are dozens of technical indicators that provide readings for assisting in short term, mid term, long term and stop loss decision-making. Decisions should not be made based on the readings of a single indicator, but on multiple indicators in order to formulate a complete market timing strategy. This report will focus on what, in the author's opinion, are the six most significant indicators. Technical indicators are viewed as mechanisms for fine-tuning hedging activity, not as absolute signals for directional trading.

The methods by which technical indicators process market data and present their analytical results fall into six groups: (1) simple averages, (2) exponential averages, (3) statistical probabilities, (4) volatility behavior, (5) price movements, and (6) money flows.

Interpreting market data in its original number format is difficult. The graphs that technical indicators provide convert number data into visual representations of price activity, making it easier to understand the causes for price movement.

The Rules, In Order Of Importance:
(1) Make profits only through a sale, never a purchase.
(2) Always apply hedges to investment or position dollars.
(3) Always apply stop losses to investment or position trades.
(4) Trade diversified instruments with high levels of trading volume.
(5) Verify indicator readings with at least two other indicators.
(6) Never trade directionally on indecisive indicator readings.
(7) Never deviate from these Rules.

E-MA (Exponential Moving Average)

Through the use of two moving average lines that smooth data, the Exponential Moving Average graph below gives extra weight to recent price data, allowing for the identification of price trends faster than can be identified by a Simple Moving Average graph.

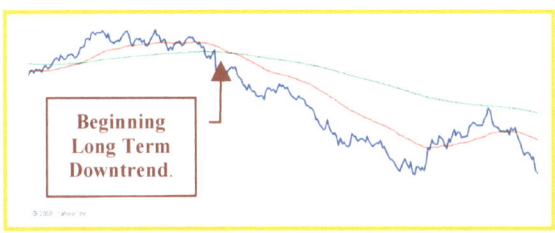
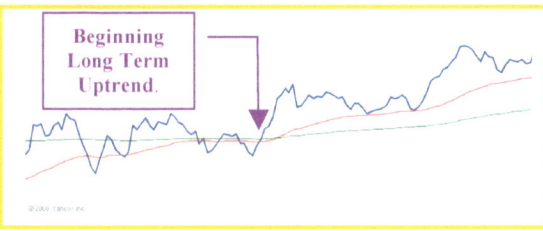

Reproduced with permission of Yahoo! Inc. ©2010 Yahoo! Inc.
YAHOO! and the YAHOO! logo are registered trademarks of Yahoo! Inc.

…an investing newsletter of general, impersonal and indirect opinion

Indicator Components
1. A line representing a 50-day (**red** line) moving average processed with an exponential weighting
2. A line representing a 200-day (**green** line) moving average processed with an exponential weighting

<u>Visual Cue</u>
❖ The red line crosses the green line.

<u>Bull Market Trend</u>
• The faster responding 50-day moving average red line crosses above the slower responding 200-day moving average green line.

<u>Bear Market Trend</u>
• The faster responding 50-day moving average red line crosses below the slower responding 200-day moving average green line.

MACD (Moving Average Convergence Divergence)

The Moving Average Convergence Divergence (MACD) indicates trend reversal, oversold or overbought sentiment, and trend strength. A zero line dividing the MACD graph on this and the following page indicates trend strength. When the blue line rises above the zero line a strong uptrend exists. When the blue line falls below the zero line it indicates a strong downtrend.

Drawn from the zero line, a histogram of convergence and divergence ticks represents the distance that the period (either daily, weekly or monthly) closing prices reside above or below the period low or high prices, respectively. A histogram with long ticks relative to average tick length indicates that the security is in an overbought state (above zero line) or oversold state (below zero line). These ticks do not have to be correlated with the blue or red line movements, but when the ticks stop lengthening from the zero line, the

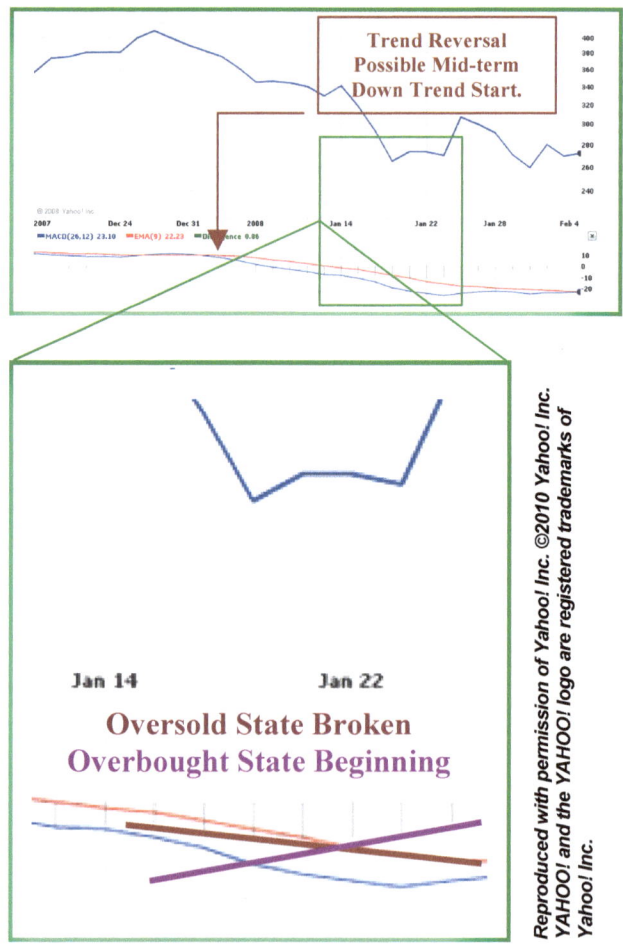

trend is weakening and the overbought or oversold states have been broken, suggesting an approaching trend reversal.

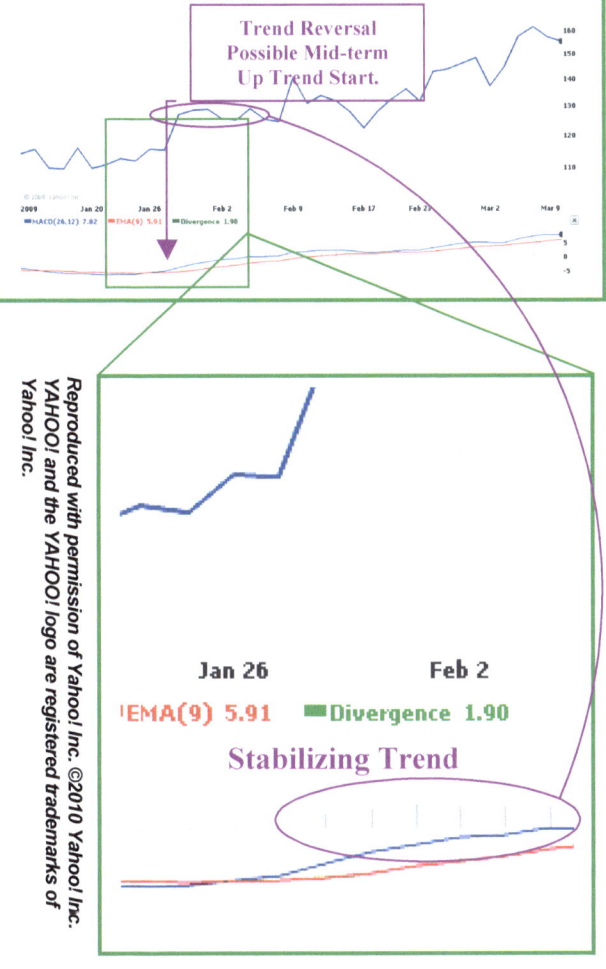

Indicator Components

1. A line representing the difference between a 26-day and a 12-day (**blue** line) Exponential Moving Average line
2. A line representing a 9-day (**red** line) Exponential Moving Average line
3. Tick marks rising and falling from the zero line

Visual Cue

❖ The **blue** line crosses the **red** line.
❖ The **blue** line crosses the zero line.
❖ The histogram ticks begin to shorten, converging toward the zero line.

Bull Market Trend

- The faster responding 26:12-day moving average **blue** line crosses above the slower responding 9-day moving average **red** line.
- The 26:12-day moving average **blue** line crosses above the zero line.
- The histogram ticks below the zero line begin to shorten, converging toward the zero line.
- The histogram ticks above the zero line begin to lengthen, diverging from the zero line.

Bear Market Trend

- The faster responding 26:12-day moving average **blue** line crosses below the slower responding 9-day moving average **red** line.
- The 26:12-day moving average **blue** line crosses below the zero line.
- The histogram ticks above the zero line begin to shorten, converging toward the zero line.
- The histogram ticks below the zero line begin to lengthen, diverging from the zero line.

Be advised that the trend strength in overbought or oversold states can be revived by security specific news or broad market sentiment. It is equally important to consider the readings on broad market indicators like the TED Spread and the VIX for sentiment direction (discussed later). Each security has its own typical histogram tick lengths based on price volatility (also defined as price amplitude) of the security. Note the examples of market price amplitude below.

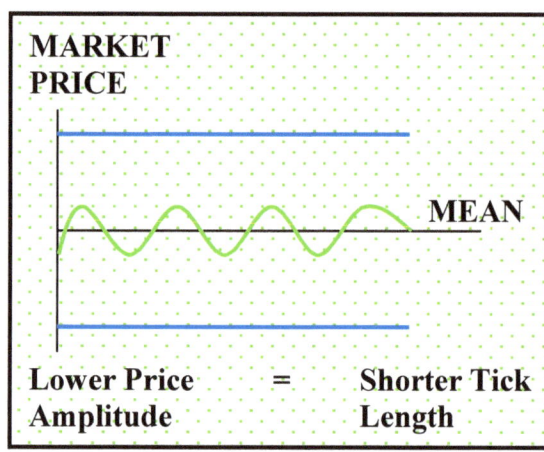

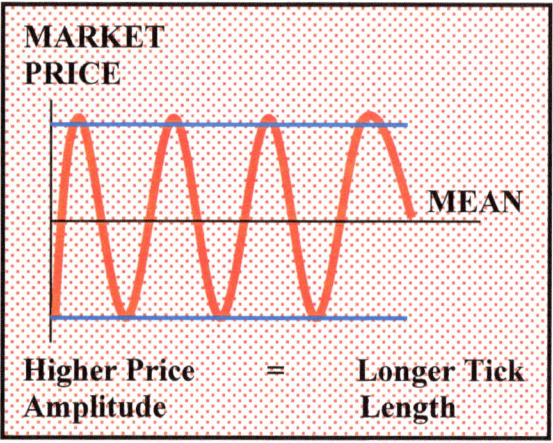

Stochastic (Oscillator)

There are both fast and slow stochastic graphs. A fast stochastic graph (not shown) is very reactive to price changes and more likely to produce false readings. The slow stochastic graph located on the following page is smoothed to reduce the choppiness seen in a fast stochastic graph. An explanation of the slow stochastic graph follows.

The theory behind oscillating indicators is that in markets that trend up, prices will tend to close nearer to the period high (day, week or month) as compared to the entire period trading range. In downward trending markets, prices will tend to close nearer to the period low as compared to the entire period trading range. The closer the closing price is to the period high or low represents greater strength of the trend up or down respectively. When closing prices move away from the period high or low extremes, the trend is weakening, signaling a reversal.

Please see page 22, for the explanation of the OHLC (Open High Low Close) charting style that supports the stochastic theory.

<u>Indicator Components</u>
1. A line representing a 5-day (**blue** line) Exponential Moving Average line
2. A line representing a 15-day (**red** line) Exponential Moving Average line

<u>Visual Cue</u>
❖ The **blue** line crosses the **red** line.
❖ Either line touches or crosses a specific graph level (i.e. 20 or 80).

Bull Market Trend
- The faster responding 5-day moving average **blue** line crosses above the slower responding 15-day moving average **red** line.
- The 5-day moving average **blue** line meets or rises above the graph level 20 line from a level below it.

Bear Market Trend
- The faster responding 5-day moving average **blue** line crosses below the slower responding 15-day moving average **red** line.
- The 5-day moving average **blue** line meets or falls below the graph level 80 line from a level above.

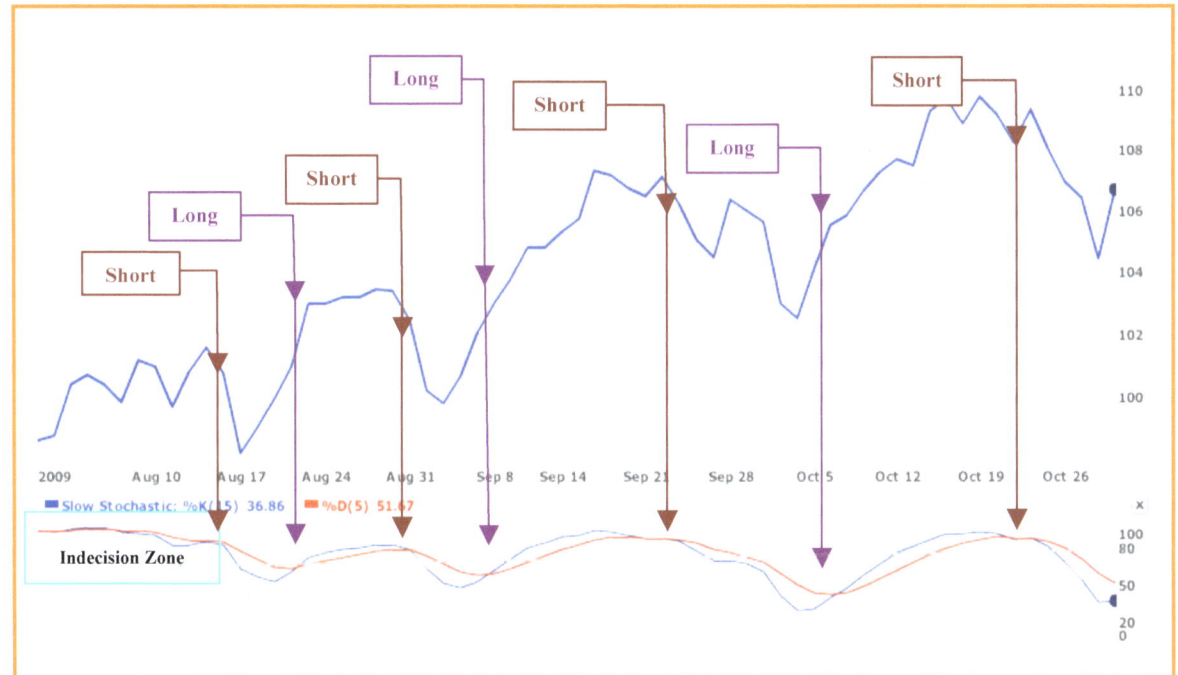

The Essential Stop Loss--Its Value And Use

The most important element of the market-timing arsenal is the stop loss. In the slow stochastic graph above, long and short entry locations are not maximized solely by the change in market sentiment from bullish to bearish and vice-versa. Rather the opportunity to maximize profit occurs by exiting the investment/position prior to the sentiment change. This is the *optimal exit point. How is the optimal exit point achieved?* It is achieved with a trailing stop-loss.

What Is A Stop Loss

Designed to limit inevitable losses when a trader is unable to constantly monitor the security, the stop loss is an instruction requesting that a security be sold (for investments) or bought (for positions) when it reaches a particular price. The price is static (non-moving) and is established through either a percentage difference or a specified dollar amount difference from the security's entering or current market value.

Stop losses are designated as market orders (taking the next available price) or limit orders (taking only a specific price). When stop losses are set as limit orders, there is a risk that the sale (for investments) or purchase (for positions) may not be fulfilled because the security's market price has moved through or around the limit price.

At what percentage or value difference should the stop loss be set from the current market price of a security? A technical indicator graph called the Parabolic Stop And Reversal (PSAR) is available that plots reliable stop loss locations through probability analysis that concludes the stop loss will not be activated by average trading range (ATR) price amplitude activity, but rather only through an identifiable trend reversal.

The Trailing Stop Loss

The trailing stop loss moves with the market price of a security (the investment) when profitable, but stands firm and ready to be activated when the market price of a security moves in an unprofitable manner. Suppose one wants to dedicate less attention to an investment/position that requires daily monitoring and adjusting of stop losses. The solution is to

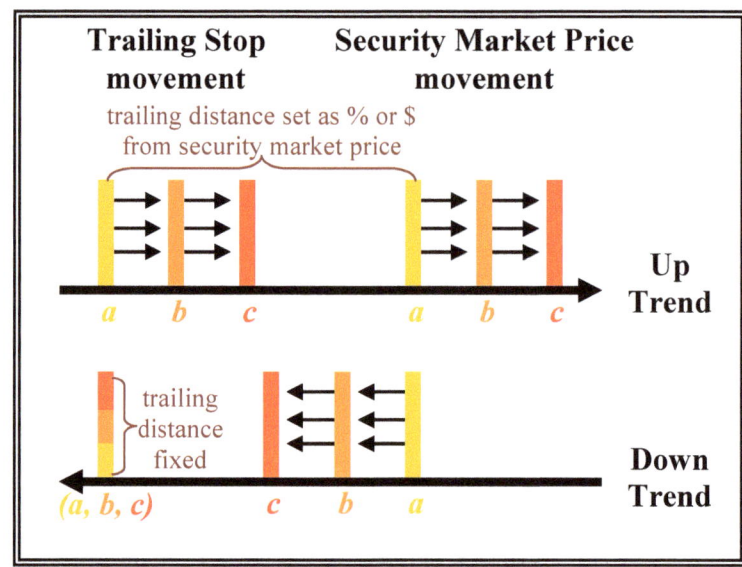

use the *trailing stop loss*, a derivation of the stop loss that tracks price movements of the security, moving with the security when it makes a favorable movement, and remaining in place as a stop loss when the security incurs an unfavorable movement. Trailing stops can be set at a percentage difference or dollar difference from the current price of a security.

The benefit of a trailing stop loss is that it realizes profits (preventing losses) sooner, rather than later, if the price of a security moves in an unfavorable direction. When activated, the trailing stop loss can be instructed to transact the security at a market price, or at a limit price (if the limit value is established and holds at the security market price when the trailing stop loss activates).

Parabolic SAR (Stop And Reversal)

Meeting two objectives in market timing, the PSAR (Parabolic Stop And Reversal) displays changes in price trends and recommended stop-loss points for the exit price of an investment or position.

Referring to the graph below, the price trend change occurs when the dots move from below or above the security price line. Dots below the price line indicate an uptrend. Dots above the price line indicate a downtrend. These dots correspond with the exponentially smoothed moving average based stop loss prices, sitting farther from the price line earlier in the trend and closer to the price line as the trend matures. The reasoning behind this placement of stop loss points is that all directional price trend changes require a high degree of agreement from market participants. In other words, the effort required to consolidate this market participant consensus is so great that a reversion to the prior trend state is less likely early in the trend, but more likely later in the trend.

A security instrument with lower volume participation requires less market participant agreement to change its price trend, while a security instrument with high volume participation requires more market participant agreement to change its price trend. This difference is reflected in the volatility of the security instrument, which translates into more accurate, more stable and less frequent price trend changes--the reason behind Rule #4: **Trade diversified instruments with high levels of trading volume.**

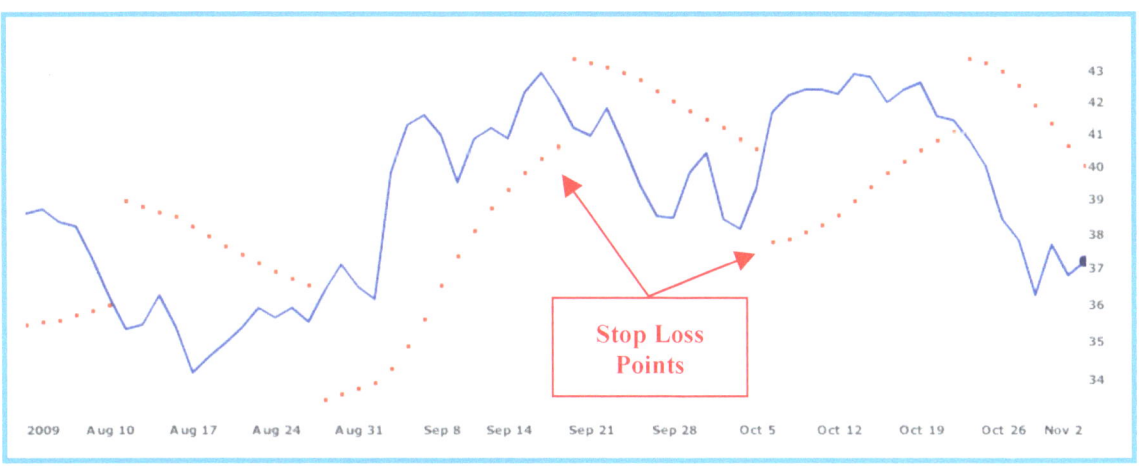

Reproduced with permission of Yahoo! Inc. ©2010 Yahoo! Inc.
YAHOO! and the YAHOO! logo are registered trademarks of Yahoo! Inc.

Indicator Components
   1. **Dots** representing an exponentially smoothed recommended stop-loss price point.
Visual Cue
   ❖ The **dots** move from below to above the price line and vice-versa.
   ❖ The **dots** move closer to the price line.

Bull Market Trend
- The **dots** reside below the price line.

Bear Market Trend
- The **dots** reside above the price line.

Stop-loss Adjustment
- The **dots** move closer to the price line.

Using the indicator above as graphed from August 10 to November 2, this randomly selected security would have produced $1.58 in losses and $8.40 in gains for a net of $6.82 per share or a gain of 18.83%. Adjustments are made to this strategy's parameters to reduce the distance between stop losses and price values either mechanically through the adjustment options of the indicator or manually by applying a trailing stop loss at the edge of the *average trading range*, thus exiting from the investment or position when price movements become undesirable.

The average trading range (ATR) is an informational statistic that provides the average price range or price spread of a security over a particular time period (daily, weekly or monthly). For example, if the average trading range reading returned 2 units for a week and the entry price is 37, the security trade profile may include one of these ranges (a, b, c, in charts to the right). If the investor is long in a security, profile (b) is ideal. If the position holder is short a security, profile (c) is ideal. Success is limited if profile (a) is the result.

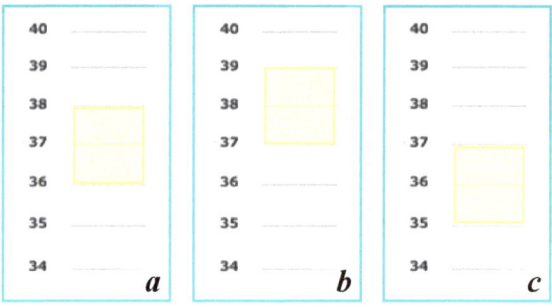

Momentum Strength (Money Flow and RSI (Relative Strength Index))
Indicator Components
1. A **trend** line graphed over a 0 to 100 range.

Visual Cue
- ❖ The **trend** line resides either below or above the 50 line.
- ❖ The **trend** line breaches the 20 or 80 line.

Bull Market Trend
- The **trend** line has breached the 20 line and is ascending toward the 50 line.
- The **trend** line resides in the 50 to 100 zone with the 50 line acting as support.

Bear Market Trend
- The **trend** line has breached the 80 line and is descending toward the 50 line.
- The **trend** line resides in the 0 to 50 zone with the 50 line acting as resistance.

Both Money Flow and RSI (Relative Strength Index) measure momentum to determine trend strength. These similar indicators suggest that the security is oversold when the trend line falls to 20 and overbought when the trend line rises to 80.

The indicator Money Flow (in graph below) uses security price and trading volume data to measure the flow of monies in or out of a security. For example, if the security price closes up, the up close is the result of money flowing into the security; if the security price closes down, it is the result of money flowing out of the security.

RSI (Relative Strength Index) measures a security's value momentum. With price as the input, RSI produces a ratio between average closing prices for up days and average closing prices for down days. It suggests the weakening of trends and coming trend reversals similar to the convergence divergence ticks of the MACD, but with a simpler single line graph.

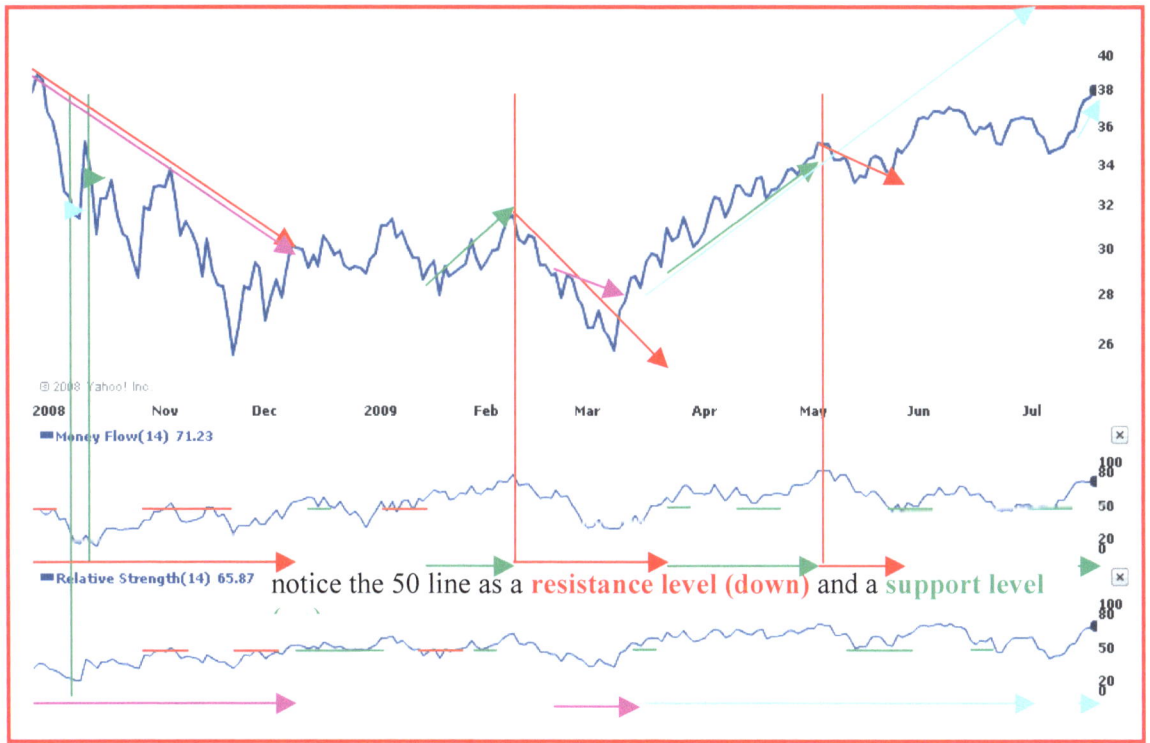

notice the 50 line as a **resistance level (down)** and a **support level**

The following visual representation taken from a mass of objects physics experiment demonstrates the relationship between momentum and trend strength. The spheres (red, yellow, green) represent varying degrees of trading volume for the Money Flow indicator and closing price averages for the RSI indicator. When pushed into a bowl, spherical objects with more mass (more trading volume and higher closing price averages) climb higher up the opposite side of a bowl than spherical objects with less mass (less trading volume and lower closing price averages); so higher money flows (as represented by trading volume) and higher price averages deliver more momentum and greater trend strength, identified by the tangential points between the price/volume momentum curve and the various spheres (red, yellow, green) representing varying degrees of trading volume for the Money Flow indicator and closing price averages for the RSI indicator.

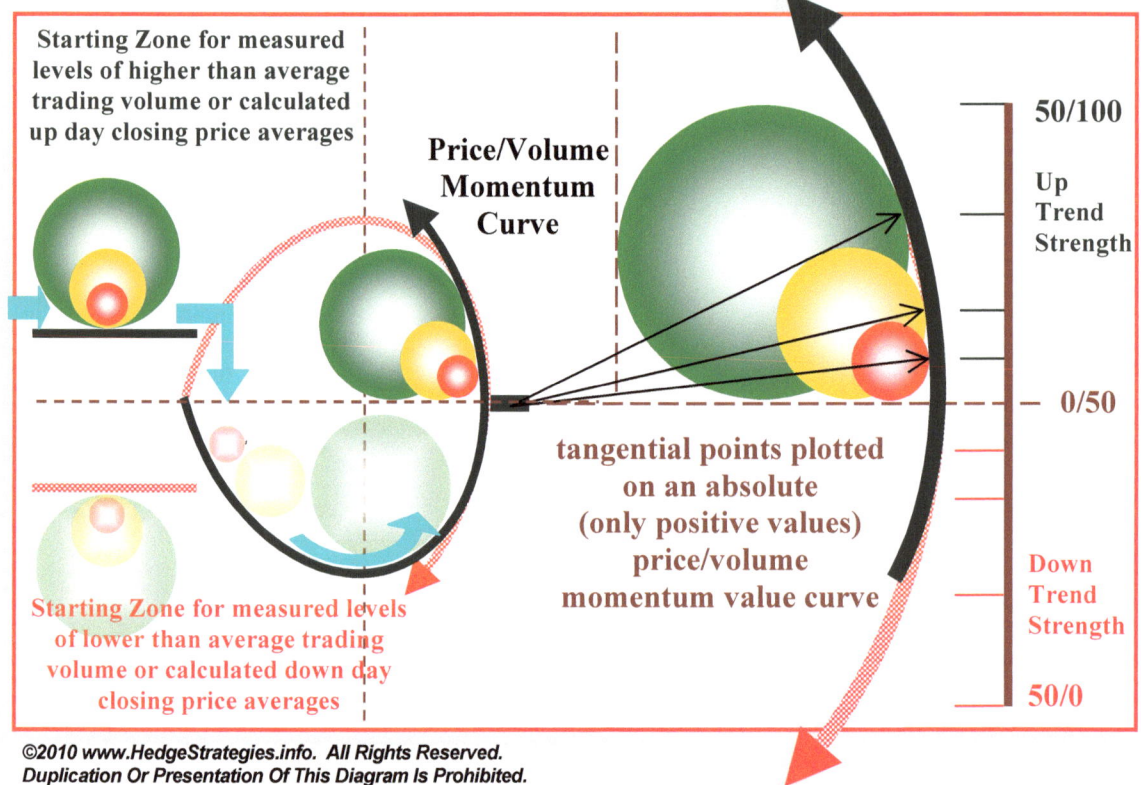

The spheres (red, yellow, green) represent varying degrees of trading volume for the Money Flow indicator and closing price averages for the RSI indicator. When pushed into a bowl, spherical objects with more mass (more trading volume and higher closing price averages) climb higher up the opposite side of a bowl than spherical objects with less mass (less trading volume and lower closing price averages); so higher money flows (as represented by trading volume) and higher price averages deliver more momentum and greater trend strength, identified by the tangential points between the price/volume momentum curve and the various spheres (red, yellow, green) representing varying degrees of trading volume for the Money Flow indicator and closing price averages for the RSI indicator.

Bollinger Bands
The most dynamic and instructive of all indicators, Bollinger bands provide information about statistical probabilities for future price ranges, possible trend reversals, a view of security price volatility and an indicator for stop loss placement.

Statistical probabilities of one standard deviation (two, three and four standard deviations may also be set in the indicator parameters) identify a range of likely price movements delineated by the green lines on either side of a red 20-day simple moving average price line. A rise in volatility is signified by spreading deviation lines.

Entry and exit points (security buy and sell signals) occur when the blue price line bounces off one of the green deviation lines. If the blue price line bounces from one green deviation line and breaks through the red moving average line, it will likely continue to the opposite green deviation line indicating a strong trend.

Stop loss and trailing stop loss instructions can be put in place when the blue price line intersects with the red moving average line. The red moving average line is resistance for an uptrend and support for a downtrend. One of two conditions will occur at this intersection point. The price line will break through the resistance or support represented by the red moving average line, which is favorable if that is the desired result, negating the need for a stop loss to exit the investment or position if the decision rendered from the technical analysis is correct. The alternative result is that the price line does not break through the resistance or support represented by the red moving average line, which is undesirable and could result in loss if precautions are not in place to exit or reverse the investment or position through use of a stop loss. The stop loss is a free precaution and should always be used.

A trend is strengthened when the blue price line breaks through a green deviation line, followed by a limited reversal with a bounce from the green deviation line acting as support (uptrend: see visualization to the right), or resistance (downtrend), and the green deviation lines diverge.

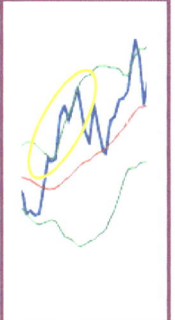

Indicator Components
1. A red line representing the 20-day simple moving average or a 20-day closing security price average.
2. A blue price line.
3. Two green deviation lines.

Visual Cue
❖ The price line (blue line) touches a deviation line (green line).
❖ The price line (blue line) bounces from one deviation line (green line) to the other deviation line (green line) with a breakout through resistance (uptrend) or breakthrough of support (downtrend) represented by the simple moving average line (red line).
❖ The green deviation lines converge toward each other.
❖ The blue price line slides along a green deviation line followed by the green deviation lines diverging from each other.

Bull Market Trend
- The components (both **green** deviation lines and the **red** moving average line) flow from lower left to upper right.
- The **blue** price line slides along the upper **green** deviation line from lower left to upper right.

Bear Market Trend
- The components (both **green** deviation lines and the **red** moving average line) flow from upper left to lower right.
- The **blue** price line slides along the lower **green** deviation line from upper left to lower right.

Technical Indicators For Market Sentiment Determination: T-ED Spread

The T-ED Spread is a comparison between the risk-free and the risky interest rates. It shows the movement of monies from riskier public sector securities markets to the risk-free government fixed income market (U.S. 3-month Treasury Bills). Using the interest rate on the 3-month T-Bill as the risk-free rate and the Eurodollar London Interbank Offered Rate (LIBOR) as a proxy for all risky rates, the difference between the two rates is the T-ED Spread.

The typical T-ED spread is between .3 and .5 percent. T-ED spread results above this level indicate a flow of monies into the risk-free T-Bill and away from risky securities (including bank overnight deposits, corporate short term letters of credit, commercial paper, and credit lines).

T-ED Spread movements negatively correlate (mirror) to the movements of securities markets. Spikes in the T-ED Spread coincide with troughs in the major indices. As money flows away from public sector markets, selling pressure causes security market prices to fall.

Technical Indicators For Market Sentiment Determination: VIX

Introduced in 1993 on the S&P 100 and then converted to the S&P 500 in 2003, the ticker symbol VIX, is the measure of volatility for the S&P 500 Index. The VIX measures the implied volatility of prices on S&P 500 Index options. Implied volatility is itself a short term measure of demand driven price inflation for options, signaling the intent to hedge the index with options against loss from either long or short positions. Though typically read as a measure for possible market declines, the VIX also can signal the movement of market prices upward.

	VIX Values		Possible 30-day 68% probable percentage value movements for the S&P 500 Index	
	15	-	4.33%	
Average	19.04	-	5.50%	1990 - October 2008
	20	-	5.77%	
	40	-	11.55%	
	60	-	17.32%	
	80	-	23.09%	
High	89.53	-	25.85%	October 24, 2008

An additional calculation is applied to the VIX to determine the 30-day anticipated value movement percentage for the broad market. The resulting percentage movement can be up, down or an additive range composed of both up and down movements. The calculation produces a possible percentage value movement within the following 30 days that has a 68% chance of occurring. The chart of calculations above shows the possible percentage value movements in the Standard and Poor's 500 Index (the right column) when the VIX returns the listed values (the left column).

For example, when the Standard and Poor's 500 Index closes at 1200 and the VIX closes at 20, there is a 68% chance in the following 30 days that the Standard and Poor's 500 Index will settle within a 138 point range between 1269, 5.77% above the current price of 1200 and 1131, 5.77% below the current price of 1200.

Analysis Techniques Applied And Verified

The following chart provides four indicators graphed on the price line for the Standard and Poor's 500 Index. A portion of the chart is hidden.

What is the anticipated movement for the Standard and Poor's 500 Index from the indicator information provided on the following page?

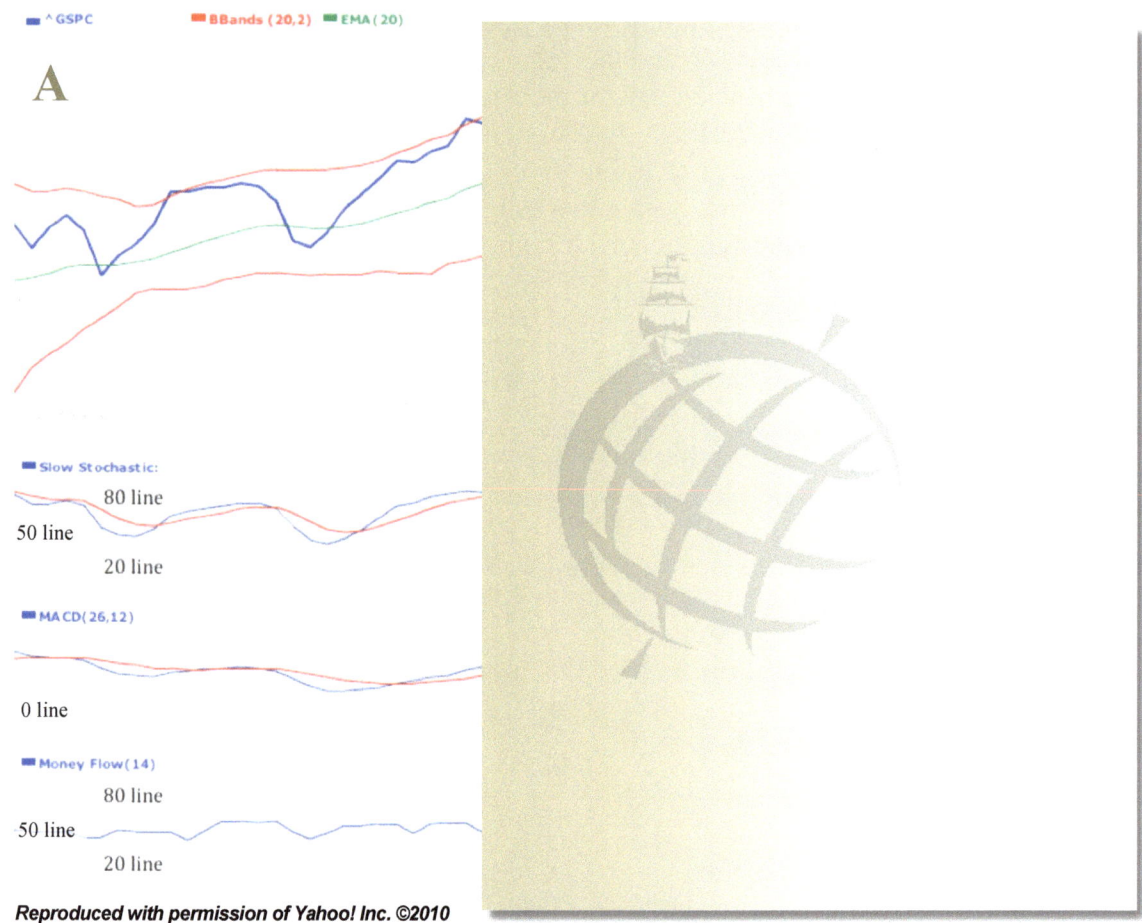

Indicator Observations From Chart (A) Above

- The **red** Bollinger bands' long term and short term trends are bullish. The **blue** price line resides in the bullish zone above the **green** moving average line and recently crossed the upper **red** deviation line. The outright breach of the upper deviation line suggests a strengthening trend. If the **blue** price line slides along the **red** upper deviation line, it will indicate a continuing uptrend.

- The slow stochastic line-pair is above the 80 line. When these lines cross, it will indicate an end to the current short term uptrend.

- The MACD resides in the bullish zone with ticks diverging. This indicates growing strength of the uptrend.

- The money flow indicator is moving toward its 50 line resistance level, but still resides in the bullish zone. If it breaks through the resistance 50 line, rather than bouncing off of resistance, it will indicate that the bullish trend is coming to an end.

Analysis From Chart (A) Above

Expect a minor correction, but not a definite end to the short term and long term bullish trends. The short term trend appears to be pausing. Favor the slow stochastic when interpreting short term activity, as other indicators experience greater lag when signaling sentiment change, making them more suited to mid term and long term interpretations.

Mid term trend reversals will be identified by crosses in the slow stochastic lines and the MACD lines, with a convergence of ticks in the MACD and a breach of the 50 line toward 0 on the money flow indicator.

Possible Action(s) Prompted From Analysis Of Chart (A) Above

The purpose and reasons for the following possible actions are thoroughly explained in the Hedge Strategies report Hedged Income Index ETF, available at the Hedge Strategies website, www.HedgeStrategies.info.

- Apply a stop loss to initiate an exit from the investment in the event that it makes a sharp downward price move.
- Establish a derivative hedge to protect the investment from loss by selling an appropriate call option.
- Order a reversing stop loss at the *hedge point* of the call option to close the call option obligation and convert the long investment into a short position.
- Order a buy stop for the hedging call option at its *theoretical maximum profit point*.

Indicator Readings Observed On Chart (B) Below

The Standard and Poor's 500 Index correction occurs at the vertical blue bar in the following graph. The slow stochastic lines have crossed and the MACD ticks have converged to the 0 line. The money flow indicator has not yet provided a definite long term trend reversing signal. Use of the possible actions from the list above would have acted to successfully secure investment profits.

Indicator Observations From Chart (B) Below

- The Bollinger bands' trend reversed from short term bullish to short term bearish when the blue price line breached the green moving average line. The red deviation lines are converging.
- The slow stochastic lines have crossed and dropped below the 80 line, also indicating a short term bearish trend. The downward steepness of the blue line is increasing.
- The MACD continues to reside in the long term bullish zone, but ticks are now diverging from the 0 line. The rate of tick divergence length from the zero line is not as steep as past tick activity, indicating that the trend is weak or non-committing.
- The money flow indicator has breached the 50 line resistance level and resides in the bearish zone, also indicating a bearish trend.

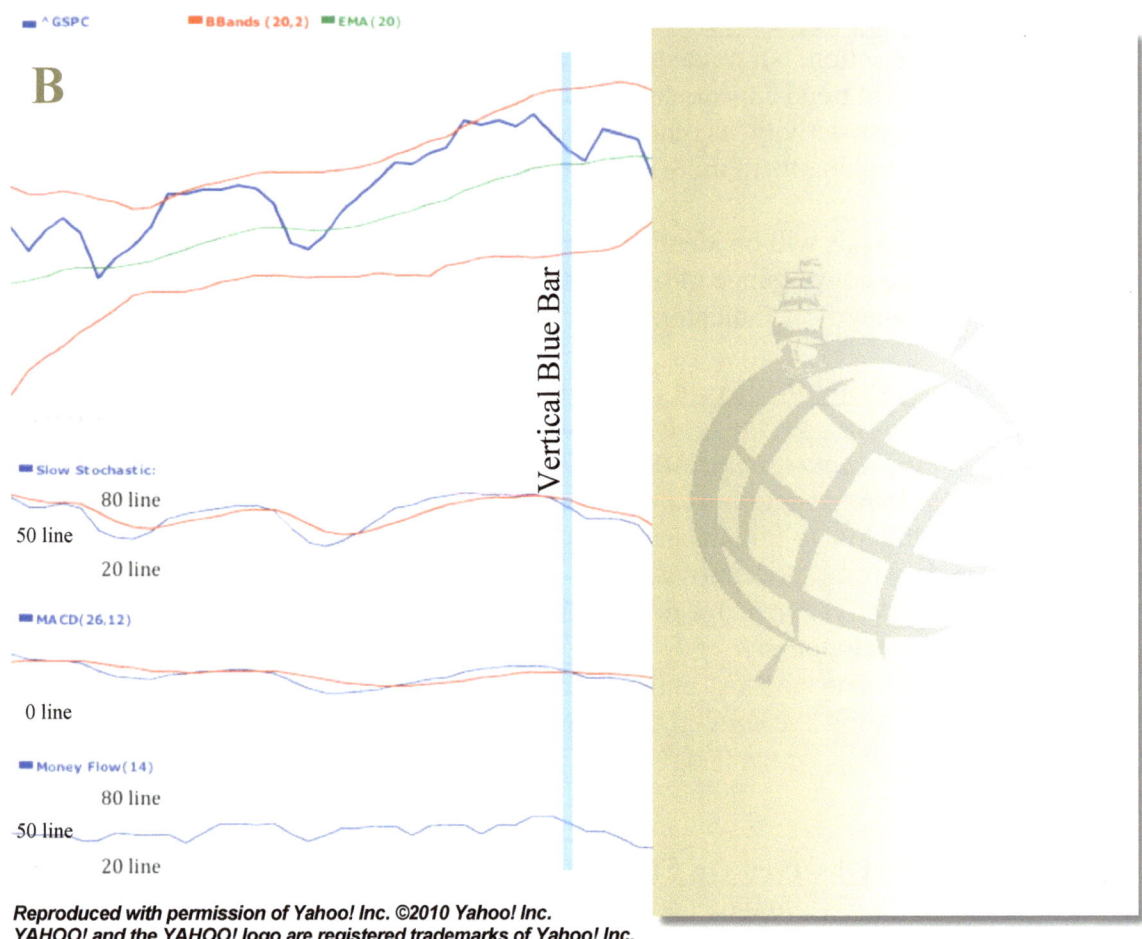

Analysis From Chart (B) Above

Expect the downtrend to continue as the slow stochastic and MACD indicators are diverging, showing downtrend momentum. The money flow confirms this move. Continued downtrend momentum can halt the long term uptrend, moving this index into a state of flat and non-committing sentiment, or a long term trend reversal. The Bollinger bands are converging which shows low volatility and stands as a warning that the short term downtrend could reverse itself. The downtrend will reverse itself if it is unable to gain a market consensus.

Possible Action(s) Prompted From Analysis Of Chart (B) Above

The purpose and reasons for the following possible actions are thoroughly explained in the Hedge Strategies report Hedged Income Index ETF, available at the Hedge Strategies website, www.HedgeStrategies.info.

- Use a stop loss set at the point where the **blue** price line crosses the **green** moving average line of the Bollinger bands indicator to defend against a short term trend reversal (from downtrend to uptrend).

- Instruct the stop loss to convert the short position to a long investment (this is one step beyond the typical stop loss instruction of simply exiting the trade).

Indicator Readings Observed On Chart (C) Below

The downtrend did not hold, and reversed itself at the vertical orange bar when the blue price line reversed and breached the resistance level established by the green moving average line. The stop loss instruction correctly reversed the short position to a long investment. The indicators confirmed this return to bullish status starting with the slow stochastic and finishing with the money flow (vertical green bars).

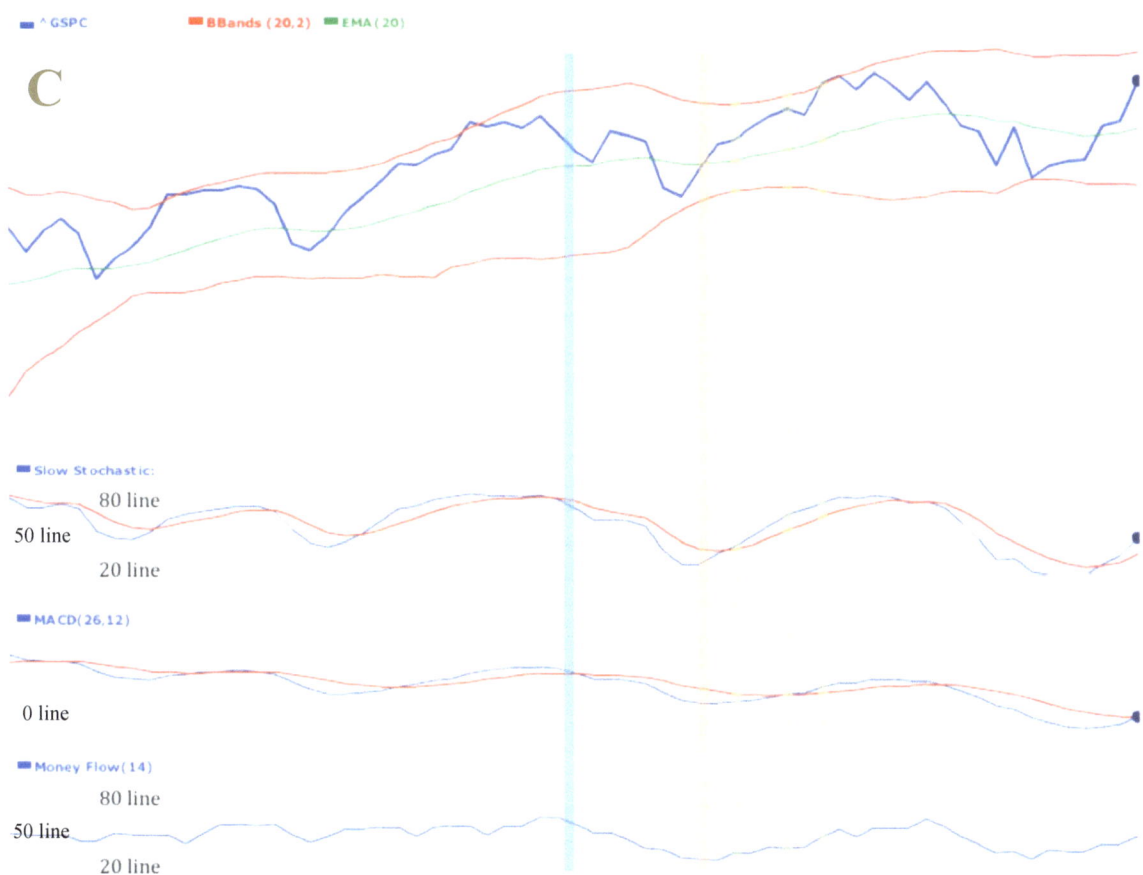

Possible Action(s) Prompted From Analysis Of Chart (C) Above

The purpose and reasons for the following possible actions are thoroughly explained in the Hedge Strategies report Hedged Income Index ETF, available at the Hedge Strategies website, www.HedgeStrategies.info.

- Use a stop loss set at the point where the blue price line crosses the green moving average line of the Bollinger bands indicator to defend against a short term trend reversal (from uptrend to downtrend).

- Convert stop loss to a trailing stop loss using either the PSAR (Parabolic Stop And Reversal) or Average Trading Range as a distance guide.

The Technical Information Found In OHLC (Open High Low Close) Charting

Stochastic oscillating theory is based on the closing location of the security price in relation to the full period (day, week or month) price range. One can gain a deeper understanding of stochastic oscillating theory by observing the pictograph price characteristics on an OHLC chart.

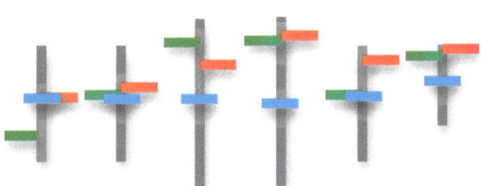

closing price
price range
average price
opening price

The OHLC pictographs to the right demonstrate a strengthening down trend because the closing price is: (1) closer to the price range lowest price than the highest price and (2) continuously below the average price value of each period.

The OHLC pictographs to the right demonstrate a strengthening up trend because the closing price is: (1) closer to the price range highest price than the lowest price and (2) continuously above the average price value of each period.

The Technical Information Found In Candlestick Charting

The shapes of period candlesticks provide directional indication (as in the following chart on page 23) and can be used to confirm technical indicator readings.

 A full candlestick with little to no tail indicates a peak in trend certainty and strength.

 A tail at the bottom of the candlestick represents buying activity or up trend strength.

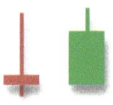 A tail at the top of the candlestick represents selling activity or down trend strength.

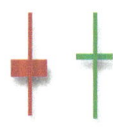 A candlestick with a shortened body and tails of nearly equal length at top and bottom shows indecision or the end of a trend.

Note in the following chart the candlestick pictographs over the price line. Observe how the indicator areas of indecision correspond to the candlestick indecision cues (in vertical **purple** outlines) and the subsequent short term reversal of prior trends.

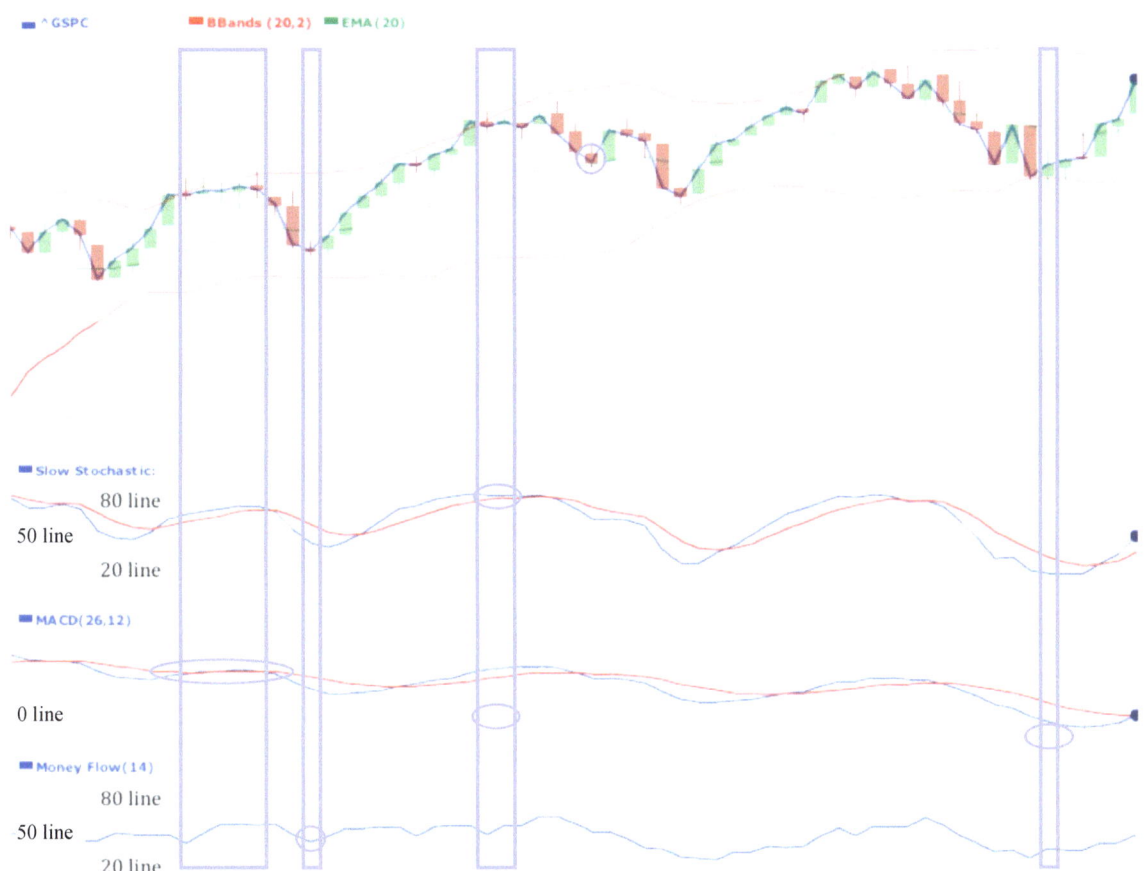

Concluding Statement

In the autumn of 2007, knowledgeable technical traders monitored market indicators that provided them with warnings for the 2008-2009 market crash and recession. They limited their exposure to market risk by removing their investments from at-risk securities and holding cash, or they hedged their investments, making money as the market fell. Detailed explanations on hedging strategies are available from Hedge Strategies reports (Hedged Income Index ETF or Hedged Short Condor Index ETF Derivative Income Spreads) available at the Hedge Strategies website, www.HedgeStrategies.info.

For those average investors who did not understand the signals provided by technical indicators in 2007 and 2008, the following years were painful.

Questions regarding this material may be forwarded to help4tat@HedgeStrategies.info.

RISK DISCLOSURE STATEMENT

It should not be assumed that concepts, models or strategies discussed, presently or in the future, will always be profitable or will equal the performance of the strategy as explained in this report.

Transactions in options carry a high degree of risk. If the option is "covered" by the seller holding a corresponding position in the underlying security or a future contract or another option, the risk may be reduced. If the option is not covered, the risk of loss can be unlimited.

Most open-outcry and electronic trading facilities are supported by computer-based component systems for the order routing, execution, matching, registration or clearing of trades. As with all facilities and systems, they are vulnerable to temporary disruption or failure. Your ability to recover certain losses may be subject to limits on liability imposed by the system provider, the market, the clearing house and/or member firms. Such limits may vary. You can ask the firm with which you deal for details in this respect.

Trading on an electronic trading system may differ not only from trading in an open-outcry market, but also from trading on other electronic trading systems. If you undertake transactions on an electronic trading system, you will be exposed to risks associated with the system including the failure of hardware and software. The result of any system failure may be that your order is either not executed according to your instructions or is not executed at all.

Additional Hedge Strategies Investment Reports

 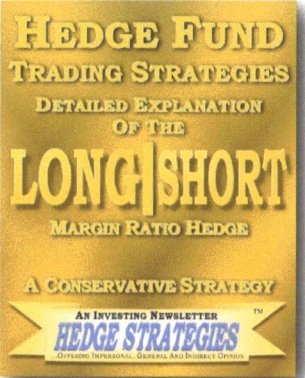 

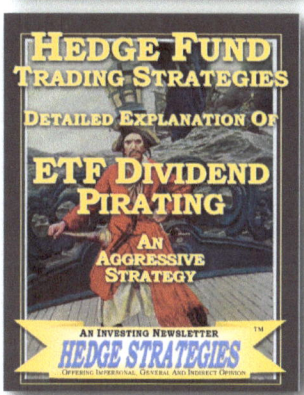 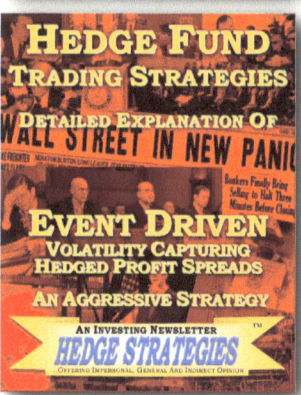 

www.ingramcontent.com/pod-product-compliance
Lightning Source LLC
Chambersburg PA
CBHW050433180526
45159CB00006B/2526